Always Precious in Our Memory

Reflections after Miscarriage, Stillbirth or Neonatal Death

Kristen Johnson Ingram

ACTA

ASSISTING CHRISTIANS TO ACT

PUBLICATIONS

Always Precious in Our Memory
Reflections after Miscarriage, Stillbirth or
Neonatal Death
by Kristen Johnson Ingram

Edited by Gregory F. Augustine Pierce
Cover Design by Tom A. Wright
Typesetting by Garrison Publications

Published by ACTA Publications
             Assisting Christians To Act
             4848 N. Clark Street
             Chicago, IL 60640
             800-397-2282

Library of Congress Catalog number: 97-72105

ISBN: 0-87946-159-4

Printed in the United States of America

01 00 99   5 4 3 2

CONTENTS

Reflections for Mothers

Reflections for Fathers

Dedicated to Jonah A. Braswell, infant,
who died December 31, 1993.
This poem by Bobbie Christensen was read
at his memorial service.

The Question

I don't understand
when a new life
is asked to detour
straight
into Christ's Presence
and not
spend time growing old on earth.

I, who am offered the longer route,
can only cry, and wait
till I too am with the Lord to ask why.

But when I stand in the awe of heaven,
will the question sit moot
upon my lips forever
while I
sing praises to God's love?

"As for me, if I am bereaved of
my children, I am bereaved."
Genesis 43:14

Introduction

It isn't possible for anyone to write a book that will take away your grief if you have lost a child to miscarriage or stillbirth or neonatal death. Even if you never saw the child you lost, your *heart* remembers, and you will always cherish his or her memory. But in this book I've tried to *share* your grief. The reflections here are just images of a grief that I have endured and that you're enduring now. Several of my reflections may help you and a few may not, but you will know you're not alone as you struggle through the next days and months.

Sometimes marriages suffer or break down after the loss of a child, usually because the couple aren't communicating their true feelings. My prayer is that you and your spouse will turn *toward* each other during this season of suffering, talking or crying or even yelling about your pain, learning to include the other's grief in your own. Please share the reflections in this book with your spouse, along with the reactions those reflections arouse.

Some well-meaning friends may advise you to forget. They probably believe that you didn't really get to know your child, and that you can erase the memory of both the expectation and the loss. They may not realize that you began to love your child the moment he or she was conceived. Perhaps this book may help you express your thoughts and feelings, the emotional flatness you may feel, or the depression that wages war with your soul.

Most of these reflections were written for both mothers and fathers of lost babies. They appear in no particular order. (There will be no easy, clear, linear "progression" to your grief—one good day can be followed by one of despair.) You will have to discover the reflection that speaks to you at any particular time.

I've also included a short section for women and one for men and a reflection for each of the four seasons. I've occasionally referred to the baby as either he and she because we're talking about real, flesh-and-blood children whose lives touched the earth like the light of a comet, and then were gone.

May God touch you with comfort and healing! Your baby, always precious in your memory, lives now with God, who wipes away the tears from every eye.

REFLECTIONS FOR THE SEASONS

AUTUMN

At first the air is crisp, trees turn gold
and crimson, and the evening is filled
with the smell of fallen leaves. But
after a month or so, those bright
leaves are gone, leaving only bare
limbs. Rain turns gardens into mud,
birds leave the country, and a lonely
wind whips around chimneys. But as
barren as this season is, I've faithfully
dropped tulip bulbs into the dark earth
because I believe that spring *will*
come again, just as I believe that
some day I'll hold my child in heaven.

> "As long as the earth endures,
>   seedtime and harvest, cold and heat,
> summer and winter, day and night,
>   shall not cease."
>
> Genesis 8:22

 WINTER

On perhaps the worst winter day of my life, when I felt as cold as the empty fields, I saw a scarlet bird pecking through the snow in my yard. I went outside, but the cardinal didn't fly away, even though I laughed aloud and thanked God for this small epiphany. I pray God will send a cardinal or bluejay or flamingo today to anyone who needs a glimpse of joy, as I did, in the midst of grief.

*For every wild animal of the forest is mine,
  the cattle on a thousand hills.
I know all the birds of the air,
  and all that moves in the field is mine.*

Psalm 50:10-11

I was so preoccupied with my grief that I didn't notice spring. The crocuses came and went and I paid no attention. Daffodils burst forth and I failed to see them. Finally, the quince bush sent up so many coral-colored blossoms in front of my window that I had to acknowledge their presence. Only then did I realize how sweet was the air, how strong the force of life blossoming in the midst of my emotional desert. Creation goes on; I can either resist or let spring into my soul.

Let us press on to know the Lord;
*   his appearing is as sure as the dawn;*
he will come to us like the showers,
*   like the spring rains that water the earth.*

Hosea 6:3

SUMMER

By the end of summer I'm ready for fall. The garden is overgrown and on the edge of deteriorating. I'm bored with my home-grown tomatoes and zucchini. Too many warm evenings have left me short-tempered and restless, my sneakers overripe from too much early morning jogging. Now I want a little friction in my life: a cold rain, an autumn leaf, a hard-to-take Bible verse.

The fading flower of its glorious beauty,
    which is on the head of those bloated with rich food,
will be like a first-ripe fig before the summer;
    whoever sees it, eats it up
    as soon as it comes to hand.

Isaiah 28:4

REFLECTIONS FOR EVERY DAY

Accusation

I was haunted by the thought that I was somehow responsible for the loss of my child. The list of my mistakes and wrongdoings was endless. Yet when I fell on my knees to confess and repent, I heard God's voice, tenderly whispering, "You did no wrong." I had forgotten that the Accuser is not God, but Someone Else.

> "Now have come the salvation and the power
> and the kingdom of our God
> and the authority of his Messiah,
> for the accuser of our comrades has been thrown down,
> who accuses them day and night before our God."
>
> Revelation 12:10

ANT BITES

I stood on an anthill when I was five, and before I could escape, red fire ants had stung me in forty or fifty places. I screamed for an hour even after my wounds were dotted with cooling ointment. My mother gathered me up and sang to me about an old man with a sack of rich gifts for me. I fell asleep in her arms. When my grief becomes unbearable, prayer takes me into the arms of Christ, who sings of the wonders in store for me.

But I have calmed and quieted my soul, like a...child with its mother.

Psalm 131:2

BATTLE

Some mornings I wake with the feeling that my grief is a battle. I rise wondering if I should strap on a sword or dress in full armor. But then I remember that God is on my side, and so are the angels, ready to vanquish the enemy of sorrow. If I step back and let God fight for my healing, I'm the winner.

"Thus says the Lord to you: 'Do not fear or be dismayed at this great multitude; for the battle is not yours but God's.'"

2 Chronicles 20:15

BLESSING

I can always find people who, when they hear about our loss, will say, "Well, it was probably a blessing." I fight my rage. They probably want to comfort me, but implying that God bestowed on us the "blessing" of our child's death is to paint a picture of a pretty awful deity. The *real* blessing has come in the form of kind friends who don't try to explain away my grief.

Blessed be the God and Father of our Lord Jesus Christ, who has blessed us in Christ with every spiritual blessing in the heavenly places.

Ephesians 1:3

BONES

My knees and ankles were throbbing and I was about ready for a cane or crutches. But although my disorder was painfully real, the doctor was certain it had been triggered by the sudden loss of our baby. The doctor gave me two prescriptions. One was for an anti-inflammatory, but the other simply said, "Talk." When I was talked out—to my spouse, to my friends, to my priest, to my parents and siblings, to anyone who would listen—my sorrow began to lift a little, and the medicine could do its work on my bones.

For my life is spent with sorrow,
And my years with sighing;
my strength fails because of misery,
and my bones waste away.

Psalm 31:10

BREATHING

"You're not trying!" my friend said. "You're giving up." But I'm still breathing, and right now that's my way of trying. It may not look like much, but it shows I'm still alive, still able to hope, still able to believe that God will speak words of tender comfort to my heart.

We are afflicted in every way, but not crushed; perplexed, but not driven to despair; persecuted, but not forsaken; struck down, but not destroyed.

2 Corinthians 4:8-9

BUSY

When her father died, my mother cleaned the house for more than a week. When my father was laid off at his job, he didn't discuss it but dug a new vegetable garden. I expected to manage my sadness the same way and was shocked to discover that keeping busy made things worse. Only when I stopped and faced my feelings did I begin to heal.

My child, do not busy yourself with many matters;
  if you multiply activities, you will not be held blameless.
If you pursue, you will not overtake,
  and by fleeing you will not escape.

Sirach 11:10

CHOICE

It would be easier on some days to curl into a little ball and then let the wind blow me across the plains. But God makes a demand on me: "Choose to live."

"Lay aside immaturity, and live, and walk in the way of insight."

Proverbs 9:6

CHRISTMAS LEFTOVER

Yesterday we moved our heavy sofa and found a sprig from our last Christmas tree. It's July now, and we're living in sorrow we didn't dream of at Christmas. I instinctively held the small dry sprig to my nose and Christmas flooded over me as my heart skipped with remembered joy. The birth of Christ signals the beginning of hope.

Then shall the trees of the forest sing for joy
    before the Lord, for he comes to judge the earth.
O give thanks to the Lord, for he is good;
    for his steadfast love endures forever.

1 Chronicles 16:33–34

COMFORT

When we came home without a baby, a score of our friends dropped by. They brought food, flowers, cards and other small gifts. They stayed to talk, to console, to encourage. But the friend I remember best is one who came and sat beside me, saying nothing at all. That friend's gift of silence was perhaps the greatest comfort I received.

> They sat with him on the ground seven days and seven nights, and no one spoke a word to him, for they saw that his suffering was very great.
>
> Job 2:13

Dawn

Some nights are so bad that the first ray of sunlight is like a reprieve. Whether I just watch a dark gray sky grow lighter by degrees or get to see the scarlet streaks of a glorious sunrise, I know the worst of the sadness is over for another day.

> Awake, my soul!
> Awake, O harp and lyre!
>   I will awake the dawn.
> I will give thanks to you, O Lord, among the peoples;
>   I will sing praises to you among the nations.
> For your steadfast love is as high as the heavens;
>   your faithfulness extends to the clouds.
>
> *Psalm 57:8-10*

EXTRAVAGANCE

They say that you should buy only what's written on your grocery list. But since my child's death, I roam the supermarket, smelling the fruit, gazing at displays, pondering the specialty counters. I sometimes buy things on impulse and often fail to bring home what I went to the store for in the first place. But although—or maybe *because*—I'm an impulse buyer, I usually bring home a bouquet of flowers or something else that is beautiful or extravagant. These things speak to our sadness in a way practical necessities never do.

My beloved speaks and says to me:
"Arise, my love, my fair one,
    and come away;
for now the winter is past,
    the rain is over and gone.
The flowers appear on the earth;
    the time of singing has come,
and the voice of the turtledove
    is heard in our land."

Song of Songs 2:10–12

FAILURE

Nobody on earth can help me, and that's a good thing. The failure of others on earth actually helps build my faith. When even my dearest friends and my spouse can't deliver me from my distress, I have to turn my eyes toward God.

> Turn, O Lord, save my life;
>   deliver me for the sake of your steadfast love....
> I am weary with my moaning;
>   every night I flood my bed with tears;
>   I drench my couch with my weeping....
> The Lord has heard my supplication;
>   the Lord accepts my prayer.
>
> Psalm 6:4,6,9

FEELINGS

"You must put the loss of your child behind you," my friend says crisply. I have to remind my friend that God made us both and is delighted in each of our personalities. Nobody can tell me how to feel...or how long to feel it.

By the grace of God I am what I am, and his grace toward me has not been in vain.

1 Corinthians 15:10

One of the tricks to hang gliding is to do *nothing*, trusting the wind to take you on your journey across the sky. But doing nothing—just letting life happen—isn't easy. Doing nothing means waiting, thinking, remembering. It feels better to stay busy, to manage, to control. If you really want to soar, however, you've got to let go and trust your life to the winds of God.

> Awake, O north wind,
>   and come, O south wind!
> Blow upon my garden
>   that its fragrance may be wafted abroad.
>
> Song of Songs 4:16

FRIENDS

I've discovered that I have several
kinds of friends who minister to me
in my grief. Some of them bring
food to the house, some drive me
to the grocery store, the doctor,
the bank. Still others clean my
stove and load my dishwasher. I
thank God for all these people. But
the friends I cherish most are the
ones who simply take me in their
arms and cry while I cry.

May your friends be like the sun
as it rises in its might.

Judges 5:37

When I took a friend's children to the fair, they were more interested in the midway than in quilts or cooking. But when I finally coaxed them to the 4-H barn to see the goats, they wanted to stay all day. One of the kids, kneeling in front of a pen of friendly, face-nuzzling goats, looked up at me and said, "My brother was wrong. You *do* know how to have fun." I apologized for my sadness and silently asked God to return to me a spirit of joy.

"This day is holy to the Lord your God; do not mourn or weep.... And do not be grieved, for the joy of the Lord is your strength."

Nehemiah 8:9, 10

GEESE

You almost never see a goose alone: they apparently know they require community. And when they're in formation, at least one other accompanies any sick or hurt goose that goes down, and they stay together until the one is healed. They never abandon each other.

Some friends play at friendship
but a true friend sticks closer than one's nearest kin.

Proverbs 18:24

GOD'S HOUSE

The local bushtits pull pale green
lichens off rocks and branches to
make their nests. Then they peck
through streambeds for white cattail
fluff to make a soft lining. God's
house, created along with me inside
my heart, has been sorely neglected.
It has been weeks since I lined it with
any soft words or refurbished it with a
prayer of adoration. Perhaps it's time
to for me to let God start rebuilding it.

> "Do not let your hearts be troubled. Believe in
> God, believe also in me. In my Father's house
> there are many dwelling places. If it were not so,
> would I have told you that I go to prepare a place
> for you? And if I go and prepare a place for you,
> I will come again and will take you to myself, so
> that where I am, there you may be also."
>
> John 14:2-3

HISTORY

I wish my antique chest could talk to me, telling me its history as a tree and then as an object used in homes long ago. At the back of a drawer, a carved label says the chest was made in 1815. I wonder about the master cabinet maker who selected the birdseye maple, bowed its front and beveled its top. Everything on earth has a precious history—even a baby that never breathed or cried or laughed. God has written that child's story in the book of life.

"You will be clothed like them in white robes, and I will not blot your name out of the book of life; I will confess your name before my Father and before his angels."

Revelation 3:5

INEDIBLE COOKIES

My neighbor had baked flower-shaped cookies, then iced and shellacked them to hang on a tree for her spring luncheon. She had to tell her son that the cookies were inedible. "You made cookies I can't eat?" he cried with disbelief, his eyes filling. Sometimes I feel as if life has nothing for me but inedible cookies, but surely God won't offer me a stone if I ask for bread...or grief when I pray for comfort.

"Ask, and it will be given you; search, and you will find; knock, and the door will be opened for you. For everyone who asks receives, and everyone who searches finds, and for everyone who knocks, the door will be opened. Is there anyone among you who, if your child asks for bread, will give a stone?"

Matthew 7:7-9

INTERCESSION

Many people have told me, "We're praying for you." That thought always makes my heart leap. I'm awed and grateful that they care enough to share my grief and ask God's help for *me*.

For this reason, since the day we heard it, we have not ceased praying for you and asking that you may be filled with the knowledge of God's will in all spiritual wisdom and understanding.

Colossians 1:9

INVITATION

When I opened the mail, I found an invitation to a party. I couldn't remember the last time my spouse and I dressed up and went out to mix with other people socially. At the thought of it, my heart cried out, "I can't!" But I did hear our friends' invitation to begin to let go of my grief, and I vowed to call just *one* other couple to come for dinner at our home. That's at least a beginning.

> "On that day, says the Lord of hosts, you shall invite each other to come under your vine and fig tree."
>
> Zechariah 3:10

KINDNESS

I had dreamed of doing a million tiny things for my daughter. I would read to her every night. I would always answer her questions honestly. I would even be nice to the callow boyfriends she would bring home some day. Instead, the only kindnesses I get to perform for her are my prayers...along with the flowers and balloons I leave on the tiny plot of earth where she lies.

Give graciously to all the living;
   do not withhold kindness even from the dead.
Do not avoid those who weep,
   but mourn with those who mourn.

Sirach 7:33–34

LEFT BEHIND

The worst thing about death is that it leaves the living behind. Maybe that's why I feel so angry about my loss: I have no control over it. I can't follow my son. He's somewhere else, doing something I don't know about. I have to wait for my life to live itself out before I see him again.

> Simon Peter said to him, "Lord, where are you going?" Jesus answered, "Where I am going, you cannot follow me now; but you will follow afterward."
>
> John 13:36

LIVING ON GRIEF

My spouse handles grief and depression by eating, but I can hardly swallow a piece of toast and a cup of tea. I'm pouring my life *out.* When I'm empty, maybe I'll be hungry again, but right now everything I try to eat is seasoned with sorrow.

My tears have been my food
day and night,
while people say to me continually,
"Where is your God?"
These things I remember
as I pour out my soul.

Psalm 42:3-4

LOCUSTS

Locusts that shear a field can actually benefit it. Granted, the locusts destroy much that is good, but they can also clear the ground for *different* crops. I guess that in God's kingdom, nothing is wasted. Madness is transformed to reason, grief to dancing, water to wine, destruction to new life.

O children of Zion, be glad
    and rejoice in the Lord your God;
for he has given the early rain for your vindication,
    he has poured down for you abundant rain,
    the early and the later rain, as before.
The threshing floors shall be full of grain,
    the vats shall overflow with wine and oil.
I will repay you for the years
    that the swarming locust has eaten.

Joel 2:23-25

LOVE

I use the word "love" pretty loosely.
I say I "love" pepperoni pizza or
Jimmy Buffet or lilacs. I often sign
"Love you" at the bottom of notes to
mere acquaintances. I talk glibly
about "loving" my neighbor. But—for
far too short a time—I was able to
truly love my baby completely, without any thought of reciprocity, and
discovered what real love is about.

*We will exult and rejoice in you;
   we will extol your love more than wine;
rightly do they love you.*

Song of Songs 1:4

MALE AND FEMALE

Male and female are obviously God's plan for the earth. Everything from plants to human beings are interdependent with the other gender. But when you live with the pain and sorrow of losing a child, it's easy to forget. Our marriage came close to breaking up because we grieved in silence, isolated from each other. Only when we came together to express our anger and sorrow to each other did we begin to heal and become one flesh again.

Then the man said,
  "This at last is bone of my bones
    and flesh of my flesh;
  this one shall be called Woman,
    for out of Man this one was taken."
Therefore a man leaves his father and his mother and clings to his wife, and they become one flesh.

Genesis 2:23-24

 MYSTERY

In my journal many years ago, I wrote a line by the novelist Katherine Mansfield. It says, "So suffering must become love. That is the mystery." Just how do I turn my suffering into love? The answer to this mystery hangs on the cross.

He has made known to us the mystery of his will, according to his good pleasure that he set forth in Christ.

Ephesians 1:9

NURSERY WINDOW

I walk down the hospital corridor trying not to glance in the nursery window. Others pause to look at their healthy babies, pointing them out to family and friends. After all the visitors have left, I stop and gaze past the row of sleeping infants and into an empty bassinet. Suddenly, I'm consumed by love for our lost baby, and I realize that love doesn't stop with death. It continues forever.

It bears all things, hopes all things, endures all things. Love never ends.

1 Corinthians 13:7-8

Oatmeal

I've always attributed my preference for oatmeal at breakfast to my Scottish ancestors, but the truth is that oatmeal reminds me of my childhood. Since the death of the baby, I find that oatmeal somehow comforts me in my loss. A loving God was preparing me, even as a child, to deal with this pain.

"You gave your good spirit to instruct them, and did not withhold your manna from their mouths, and gave them water for their thirst. Forty years you sustained them in the wilderness so that they lacked nothing."

Nehemiah 9:20-21

PASSION FLOWERS

The intricate white blooms that
come from my neighbor's vine are
called "passion flowers" because the
blossom is supposed to symbolize
events in the Passion of Christ. The
little purple corona stands for the
crown of thorns, the styles represent
the nails used in the Crucifixion, and
the stamens are for the five wounds.
I wish I could symbolize my grief in
the form of a flower, so that everyone who saw it would understand my
sorrow...without my having to tell
the story again.

> This is a symbol of the present time.
>
> Hebrews 9:9

PATIENCE

I don't know whether all my friends have suddenly become brainless or what, but I don't think I can stand to hear once more, "Well, it was probably for the best," or "Your baby is in a better place than this world." In their own sorrow and discomfort, ordinarily intelligent, sensitive people around me have lost the ability to talk sense. I have to remember to take a deep breath and have patience with them. We are all just sojourners on earth, and we're all learning about life as we travel along together.

We urge you, beloved, to admonish the idlers, encourage the faint hearted, help the weak, be patient with all of them. See that none of you repays evil for evil, but always seek to do good to one another and to all.

1 Thessalonians 5:14–15

Our parish church started collecting to create a "mile of pennies" for a mission project—with no other coins accepted. I began hoarding pennies for the church. In the same way, I'm trying to hoard tiny scraps of joy and peace for myself. Sometimes happiness lasts only a few seconds, and contentment barely flashes through my consciousness. But eventually I'll have a whole mile of rejoicing.

> *Weeping may linger for the night, but joy comes with the morning.*
>
> *Psalm 30:5*

PHOTOGRAPH

When you develop a color photo, you go through a process where the red, yellow and blue layers create the picture. Greens and browns appear. Trees put out leaves. Skies go from bright blue to sunset hues. But something is still missing until you add the black. Then the shapes are complete and the shadows have dimension. In the same way, my grief has added depth and even richness to my person.

"I have set my rainbow in the clouds, and it shall be a sign of the covenant between me and the earth."

Genesis 9:13

PLEASURE

I know that humans were made for happiness, but sometimes I have to *practice* feeling pleasure again. I try to take new joy in small things: a cup of fragrant coffee in a delicate porcelain cup, a colorful leaf blown against the window, a good book or movie. As I practice deliberate pleasure, my spirit responds with little surges of delight and I start to become whole again.

> You show me the path of life.
> In your presence there is fullness of joy;
> in your right hand are pleasures forevermore.
>
> Psalm 16:11

POMEGRANATE

I was eating sweet pomegranate seeds, picking out the juicy crimson bits with a fork, when I accidentally got a piece of the white membrane in my mouth. How, I wondered, can anything so bitter contain such sweetness? Maybe someday I'll look back on these painful days as a time of renewal and refreshment, a time when God spoke to me through my tears.

How sweet are your words to my taste,
  sweeter than honey to my mouth!
Through your precepts I get understanding;
  therefore I hate every false way.
Your word is a lamp to my feet
  and a light to my path....
I am severely afflicted;
  give me life, O Lord according to your word.

Psalm 119:103–105, 107

PORCUPINE

My headlights focused on a porcupine who was lumbering across the dark country road. As I put on my brakes he stopped too, looking straight at me. I think if he had arms and hands like ours, he might have saluted before he resumed his waddling journey. I'm in God's headlights right now. God sees my sorrow and inner turmoil and holds me for a moment, waiting for me to resume my life journey.

I sought the Lord, and he answered me,
and delivered me from all my fears....
This poor soul cried, and was heard by the Lord,
and was saved from every trouble.

Psalm 34:4,6

PRAYER

My eight-year-old niece tossed a coin into the fountain. "I hope my wish comes true," she said. "I wished for a pet bunny." Now, my niece lives on the sixteenth floor of an apartment building in New York City. There's no way she can have a live rabbit, no matter how much she hopes or how many coins she tosses down a wishing well. Sometimes I feel that my prayer is like my niece's wish: God never says no, exactly, but the result prayed for is impossible.

For God alone my soul waits in silence,
 for my hope is from him.
He alone is my rock and my salvation,
 my fortress; I shall not be shaken.
On God rests my deliverance and my honor;
 my mighty rock, my refuge is in God.

Psalm 62:5-7

Remembering

Janet and Leland had their son for sixteen years before he died. They wanted desperately to make sense of their loss and make sure the world remembered their son. So they donated millions of dollars to start Stanford University. I don't have millions to contribute in my son's memory, and most of the world probably won't remember him. I have given my heart, instead, and there he will never be forgotten.

Remember that you fashioned me like clay....
You clothed me with skin and flesh,
   and knit me together with bones and sinews.
You have granted me life and steadfast love,
   and your care has preserved my spirit.

Job 10:9, 10

RISK

In the computer game *Centipede*, I fire my "bug-zapper" at colorful centipedes, scorpions, spiders and fleas. At each level the game becomes more difficult. Because I take wild risks I sometimes lose—but more often I score high.   Maybe I can still risk living fully if God will remain at my side, hand on the controls with mine.

Not by their own sword did they win the land,
*   nor did their own arm give them victory;*
but your right hand, and your arm,
*   and the light of your countenance,*
*   for you delighted in them.*

Psalm 44:3

ROCK

I keep a piece of quartz on my desk.
It looks pretty ordinary until you
look at the lower right corner,
where a dark red garnet the size of
a dime juts out of the milky crystal.
If you turn the rock over, you find
that the quartz is covering a piece
of pyrite that's studded with tiny
garnets. That's how I think about
my daughter—a beautiful jewel now
hidden in the rock of death.

> There is gold, and abundance of costly stones;
> but the lips informed by knowledge are a precious jewel.
>
> Proverbs 20:15

Running

My hometown has several half-marathons and 10-K races every year. Some who enter are serious runners, some beginners. A number of people in wheelchairs participate. Only one person can win each race, but most people's goal is to *finish* the course. I know that Christ has a crown of righteousness for me if I but finish this marathon of sorrow in faith.

I have fought the good fight, I have finished the race, I have kept the faith. From now on there is reserved for me the crown of righteousness, which the Lord, the righteous judge, will give me on that day, and not only to me but also to all who have longed for his appearing.

2 Timothy 4:7-8

SARCASM

By late afternoon, nobody at my office was speaking to me because of my snappishness and sarcastic remarks. I remembered that the literal meaning of sarcasm is "to tear the flesh apart." I had to go from desk to desk, apologizing; I received grace and forgiveness from everyone I spoke to, just as I receive it from God when I confess my bad moods as sin and stop trying to attribute them to my grief.

Be angry, but do not sin; do not let the sun go down on your anger, and do not make room for the devil.

Ephesians 4:26-27

SHAPING THE SOUL

The Irish poet Seamus Heaney, who received the Nobel Prize for literature, said somewhere that we have to be knocked around some because it's living that shapes the soul. Once I would have said my soul was shaped like a soaring bird. Today it feels like a heavy, gray rock. I wonder what God sees, looking at me.

How long, O Lord? Will you forget me forever?
How long will you hide your face from me?
How long must I bear pain in my soul,
and have sorrow in my heart all day long?

Psalm 13:1–2

SHOCK

Today I was shocked back into reality. One of my closest friends called to share that he had been diagnosed with terminal cancer. I was amazed to discover that I felt angry. I wanted to shout, "I don't have *time* for this! You know I'm busy grieving for my child!" But instead I rushed to his side, leaving my own grief unattended for a while.

> "As your life was precious today in my sight, so may my life be precious in the sight of the Lord, and may he rescue me from all tribulation."
>
> 1 Samuel 26:24

SNEAKERS

My running shoes were falling apart. One tongue was gone, the shoestrings were broken, the soles were fast pulling away from the upper parts. I resisted getting new ones. I wanted as few new things in my life as possible after the death of my child. But when I finally began bruising my heels, the doctor sent me to buy new shoes. Resisting change—even change that heals—is hard. But I'm beginning to realize that if I'm not willing to let go of my old spiritual shoes, my soul might be bruised permanently.

How beautiful upon the mountains
*   are the feet of the messenger who announces peace,*
who brings good news,
*   who announces salvation,*
*   who says to Zion, "Your God reigns."*

                                    Isaiah 52:7

Snow

Sometimes I'd like to shovel away the snow of my daily life and give in to my grief forever. But it is my everyday activity that shelters me from the freezing cold of sadness.

Praise the Lord, O Jerusalem!
Praise your God, O Zion!
For he strengthens the bars of your gates;
*   he blesses your children within you.*
He grants peace within your borders;
*   he fills you with the finest of wheat.*
He sends out his command to the earth;
*   his word runs swiftly.*
He gives snow like wool;
*   he scatters frost like ashes.*

Psalm 147:12–16

STARVING

We had such a freeze last Christmas that birds couldn't even turn over the leaves to look for food. I had to provide something, so I started chopping up bread, rolls, even the leftover Christmas *buche*. I sprinkled them on the railing of our deck and watched as chickadees, juncos, starlings and sparrows swooped onto my deck to get a little sustenance. The next Sunday as I entered my pew, I looked up at the altar and realized that I, too, was starving for the Bread of Life.

> "I am the bread of life. Whoever comes to me will never be hungry, and whoever believes in me will never be thirsty."
>
> John 6:35

STORING UP

We own a house and two cars. We have computers and printers, a scanner and a fax machine—all things that matter to our work. One of us has a few pieces of good jewelry and the other a garage full of expensive tools. But none of those things is our treasure. If they were lost or stolen or destroyed, we would be sorry but not sad. Our real treasure is in heaven, waiting to be reunited with us.

"*Do not store up for yourselves treasures on earth, where moth and rust consume and where thieves break in and steal; but store up for yourselves treasures in heaven.... For where your treasure is, there your heart will be also.*"

Matthew 6:19,21

STORM

I rushed out into the storm to drag framed vinyl sheets over my tender young tomato plants. Torrents were pouring onto my red-leafed lettuce and pea vines, and I did what I could to protect them with tarps and heavy paper. Rain, which can sometimes injure young plants, is also necessary for them to live. Perhaps the grief I feel today, which has nearly destroyed my soul, is actually necessary to make me fully alive. I just hope God will soon drag some protection over me.

Be merciful to me, O God, be merciful to me,
    for in you my soul takes refuge;
in the shadow of your wings I will take refuge,
    until the destroying storms pass by.

Psalm 57:1

SWALLOWS

Every year a pair of swallows returns to our yard. They swoop, soar, court, get remarried and build a nest under the eaves in our garage. They grow quite fierce in their protection of that nest: they threaten to peck my little dog and grow aggressive with any robin that might wander into the yard. But when their young are hatched and finally flying, they tear up the nest and let the materials fall to the cement in our patio. They know, better than I ever have, when a season is finished and a new one has to begin.

How lovely is your dwelling place,
O Lord of hosts!
My soul longs, indeed it faints
for the courts of the Lord;
my heart and my flesh sing for joy
to the living God.
Even the sparrow finds a home,
and the swallow a nest for herself,
where she may lay her young.

Psalm 84:1-3

TALKING DONKEY

The biblical story of Balaam's donkey that spoke was one of my childhood favorites— not just because an animal talked but because it argued with its master! Now I am constantly arguing with God, asking that my cross be removed.

The Lord opened the mouth of the donkey, and it said to Balaam, "What have I done to you, that you have struck me these three times? ...Am I not your donkey, which you have ridden all your life to this day? Have I been in the habit of treating you this way?" And (Balaam) said, "No."

Numbers 22:28-29

TEARS

What if we had tears for only one or two times in our lives? We'd be in constant fear of using them. Fortunately, no matter how many times or how long I cry, my body will keep manufacturing all the tears I need to express my sorrow, rage and pain at the loss of my child. I don't have to conserve my tears; I can let them flow freely now, today. They'll be there tomorrow, if I need them, and the next day, too.

You have kept count of my tossings;
put my tears in your bottle.
Are they not in your record?

Psalm 56:8

TREASURE

When I was a child I liked to search for treasure. Legend said that a horde of gold was buried in our town, and my friends and I would look for big, gnarled oak trees, pace off the ground, and start digging. Of course, we never found gold, but the real fun was in the search. Perhaps if I keep digging in the dark earth of my soul, I'll find the treasure chest that God has hidden for me.

My child, if you accept my words
*   and treasure up my commandments within you,*
making your ear attentive to wisdom
*   and inclining your heart to understanding;*
if you indeed cry out for insight,
*   and raise your voice for understanding;*
if you seek it like silver,
*   and search for it as for hidden treasures—*
then you will understand the fear of the Lord
*   and find the knowledge of God.*

Proverbs 2:1-5

VISION-IMPAIRED

I'd heard about blind anger, but I
hadn't realized how grief can also
impair our vision. I'm certain we still
have beautiful sunsets. The produce
section of the supermarket must be
piled high with colorful fruits and
vegetables. Surely, the lilacs and
peonies in my garden are as glorious
as they were last year. I just cannot
see them.

Save me, O God,
for the waters have come up to my neck.
I sink in deep mire,
where there is no foothold;
I have come into deep waters,
and the flood sweeps over me.
I am weary with my crying;
my throat is parched.
My eyes grow dim
with waiting for my God.

Psalm 69:1-3

VISIT

I like to think that if Jesus were coming to visit me I'd make vast preparations—perhaps buying him a new bed, or erecting a bower in my yard, or planting more of my famous rhododendrons. But I wonder how many times recently he's arrived unnoticed into the pathways of my heart to find them littered with bad temper and self-pity.

"In the wilderness prepare the way of the Lord,
make straight in the desert a highway for our God."

Isaiah 40:3

Yesterday I passed an amber wheat field full of tall ripe grain. That night at dinner I thought about all the things wheat goes through to become first flour and finally bread for my table. It is pounded and milled and strained; enriched, leavened with yeast, raised and punched down and raised again; then baked at a high temperature until finally transformed. Right now *I'm* in God's kitchen—being pounded and milled, leavened and raised, baked and transformed. I can only hope that when this process is finished, I'll be fit to be bread for others.

If you will only heed his every commandment that I am commanding you today—loving the Lord your God, and serving him with all your heart and with all your soul—then he will give the rain for your land in its season, the early rain and the later rain, and you will gather in your grain, your wine, and your oil; and he will give grass in your fields for your livestock, and you will eat your fill.

Deuteronomy 11:13–15

WHISKERS

We were horrified when our cat returned—after a week's absence—thin, matted and with his whiskers cut off! Someone had abused our beloved kitty. For weeks he had trouble tasting and smelling, and he spent a lot of time under our bed. He acted defeated and depressed until his whiskers grew in again. In my grief, I feel as if some absolutely vital part of me has been cut off. I can't taste or smell either, and I'd like to crawl under the bed until I grow a new heart.

A new heart I will give you, and a new spirit I will put within you; and I will remove from your body the heart of stone and give you a heart of flesh.

Ezekiel 36:26

WORDS

One friend, fumbling awkwardly for words to say, murmured, "Try to forget." If there's one thing I *don't* want to do, it's forget my child. I want to remember every detail of that little life, every miniature finger and toe, every curve of that baby-born-too-soon mouth. I cherish that brief moment when our baby cried, and I play that memory over and over in my mind. My friend meant well, but if I forget, I have nothing.

> *Set me as a seal upon your heart,*
> *as a seal upon your arm;*
> *for love is strong as death,*
> *passion fierce as the grave.*
>
> *Song of Songs 8:6*

Zoo Trip

I thought a picnic at the zoo a hundred miles from home might take my thoughts from my sorrow. But it was the season when most baby animals are born, and every animal had its cub or kit or calf. I left the place feeling more deprived than ever. But later I found myself thanking God that life does go on, that animal and human children are still being born, that God is still in control.

The Lord God formed every animal of the field and every bird of the air, and brought them to the man to see what he would call them; and whatever the man called every living creature, that was its name.

Genesis 2:19

REFLECTIONS
FOR MOTHERS

BATHTUB

When I can't stand my life any longer, I soak in our huge bathtub. I pour in bath oil or bubbles or salts, burn incense and light candles to enhance my long, leisurely bath. My husband once said he couldn't understand why anyone would want to lie in a tub full of water. "To celebrate my baptism," I told him. "It's my connection to God." Later, I found him soaking in the tub. It was the first time I'd seen him cry since our baby died.

> *You visit the earth and water it,*
> *you greatly enrich it;*
> *the river of God is full of water.*
>
> *Psalm 65:9*

BREAD

My grandmother told me that when she felt sad or angry, she would make three loaves of bread. She didn't have a bread machine in those days, of course. She said the work of kneading bread and raising it twice helped her work out her feelings. And at the end of the day, she had three hot, fragrant gifts to share with others.

You cause the grass to grow for the cattle,
    and plants for people to use,
to bring forth food from the earth,
    and wine to gladden the human heart,
oil to make the face shine,
    and bread to strengthen the human heart.

Psalm 104:14–15

CRYING

I woke in a hotel room to hear a baby crying. For a second, I thought it was my lost child, miraculously alive. But soon I realized that in some nearby room, another mother was rising in the night to feed or soothe her child. God, help me to remember that—although it feels as if the universe has stopped—life goes on around me, just as it always has, just as it always will.

> No testing has overtaken you that is not common to everyone. God is faithful, and he will not let you be tested beyond your strength, but with the testing he will also provide the way out so that you may be able to endure it.
>
> 1 Corinthians 10:13

MEMORY

I tried to remove every reminder of my loss. I sent my maternity garments, along with the new baby clothes and nursery furniture, to a charity shop. I painted the yellow walls white and hung up a Navajo rug. I put my desk back in the room, along with a couple of chairs and a magazine rack. But only when I began to offer my life back to God, did I realize that I will never—nor would I ever want to— forget my child.

All the ends of the earth shall remember
  and turn to the Lord;
and all the families of the nations
  shall worship before him.
For dominion belongs to the Lord
  and he rules over the nations.
To him, indeed, shall all who sleep in the earth bow down;
  before him shall bow all who go down to the dust,
  and I shall live for him.
Posterity will serve him;
  future generations will be told about the Lord,
and proclaim his deliverance to a people yet unborn,
  saying that he has done it.

Psalm 22:27-31

MOTHER'S DAY

Mother's Day is the hardest holiday for me. I send flowers to my own mother and cards to relatives with children. But gifts and cards don't arrive here. No matter what diversion I seek, my arms feel emptier on this day than any other. Perhaps we should have a holiday for those whose children live only in their hearts.

Her children rise up and call her happy;
her husband too, and he praises her:
"Many women have done excellently,
but you surpass them all."

Proverbs 31:28-29

SECOND DEATH

I thought when I went home
from the hospital that the worst
would be over. I hadn't counted
on how painful it would be to
have my friends and family
grieving with me. Each time a
new visitor came, I endured a
second death. But—although I
am not naturally outgoing—I
made myself talk to everyone
who came. These conversations
weren't magic, but after a while
they somehow gave me the
strength to begin to hold my
child precious in my memory.

This is the second death, the lake of fire.

Revelation 20:14

REFLECTIONS FOR FATHERS

NECKTIE

The morning of my child's funeral, I couldn't tie my necktie. I suddenly couldn't remember how to do something I'd been doing every day for thirty years. I had always prided myself on my independence, stability and strength; but now, for the first time since early childhood, I felt helpless. That moment left me with new compassion for those who respond to death with feelings of powerlessness. Now I'm able to weep with them...or help them tie their neckties.

> "Today I am powerless."
>
> 2 Samuel 3:39

SACRAMENT

As I was driving home from work one night, I began to realize I may never be a father. I wanted to pull off the freeway and let my fierce tears flow. Instead, I went home and embraced my wife. We fell into each other's arms, remembering that the sacrament God ordained is *matrimony*, not parenthood.

> Then the Lord God said, "It is not good that the man should be alone; I will make him a helper as his partner."
>
> Genesis 2:18

SPEED

When I saw the police car's lights flash I glanced down at my speedometer and saw how fast I was driving. I don't usually share my feelings easily; but when the officer approached the car and asked for my license, I blurted out, "I'm sorry. I buried my baby this morning and I was just out driving around." To my surprise, he handed back my license and said, "Go home to your wife. She needs you now."

From the depths of the earth you will bring me up again. You will increase my honor, and comfort me once again.

Psalm 71:20-21

TWO FATHERS

Ever since childhood, I had planned to be a certain kind of father: one who would be generous, show affection, play with his kids, answer all their questions. It never occurred to me that I might be a *grieving* father. Yet when I pray I hear God whispering, "My Son died, too."

For God so loved the world that he gave his only Son, so that everyone who believes in him may not perish but may have eternal life.

John 3:16

WALKING

I read that after his wife died a famous television personality lay on his hotel bed at a seaside resort. His five-year-old son begged him to walk on the beach, but the man said, "I can't." The little boy stood still for a moment and then grabbed his dad's hand. "Come on, Daddy," he said. "Walk with me until you fall down."

> *Our steps are made firm by the Lord,*
> *when he delights in our way;*
> *though we stumble, we shall not fall headlong,*
> *for the Lord holds us by the hand.*
>
> *Psalm 37:23-24*

HISTLE

When I was a boy, my father and I were camped in the mountains, fishing for trout in a rushing river. One day when nothing was biting and I was getting bored, Dad cut a six-inch stick from an elder tree. He carefully slid the bark off, carved out the inside of the twig and made several notches, then worked the bark back over it. Now I had a whistle whose tones I could change by sliding the bark over the notches. I'd hoped to take my own child fishing someday, but I know that if I make a whistle from a mountain elder, my child will still hear my song.

He will raise a signal for a nation far away,
and whistle for a people at the ends of the earth;
Here they come, swiftly, speedily!

Isaiah 5:26

ALSO FROM ACTA PUBLICATIONS

The New Day Journal
A Journey from Grief to Healing
by Sr. Mauryeen O'Brien, O.P.

A book offering those who have lost a loved one a structured way to work through the "tasks of grief," including accepting the reality of the loss, experiencing the pain of grief, adjusting to the new environment in which the deceased is missing, and moving on with life. 92 page workbook, $8.95.

From Grief to Grace
Images for Overcoming Sadness and Loss
by Helen R. Lambin

Each of the ten chapters of this sensitive book suggests several images to assist people in naming, processing and overcoming their grief. Using this collection of creative symbols, individuals can begin to comprehend their feelings of sadness and loss, and then start the process of turning their occasions of grief into opportunities for grace. 96 pages, $8.95.

The Legend of the Bells and Other Tales
Stories of the Human Spirit
by John Shea

Twenty-five of theologian and master storyteller John Shea's favorite stories, including "The Grieving Woman and the Spiritual Master." Drawn from many different religious traditions, spiritual legends and everyday experiences, each story speaks directly to the spiritual seeker's heart and mind and is followed by the author's thought-provoking explanation, which gives a practical, personal relevance to the story. 192 pages, $12.95.

AVAILABLE FROM BOOKSELLERS
OR CALL 800-397-2282